Keep this pocket-sized F
you are visiting Lincolns
in the locality.

Whether you are in your car or on foot, you will
enjoy an evocative journey back in time. Compare
the Lincolnshire of old with what you can see
today—see how the streets, parks and open spaces
have changed; examine the shops and buildings and
notice how they have been altered
or replaced; look at fine details such as lamp-posts,
shop fascias and trade signs; and see the many
alterations to Lincolnshire that have taken place
unnoticed during our lives, some of which we may
have taken for granted.

At the turn of a page you will gain fascinating
insights into Lincolnshire's unique history.

FRANCIS FRITH'S
pocket ALBUM

LINCOLNSHIRE

A POCKET ALBUM

Adapted from an original book by
MARTIN ANDREW

First published in the United Kingdom in 2005 by
Frith Book Company Ltd

ISBN 1-84589-079-5
Text and Design copyright © Frith Book Company Ltd
Photographs copyright © The Francis Frith Collection

The Frith photographs and the Frith logo are reproduced under licence from Heritage
Photographic Resources Ltd, the owners of the Frith archive and trademarks

British Library Cataloguing in Publication Data

Lincolnshire—A Pocket Album
Adapted from an original book by Martin Andrew

Frith Book Company Ltd
Frith's Barn, Teffont,
Salisbury, Wiltshire SP3 5QP
Tel: +44 (0) 1722 716 376
Email: info@francisfrith.co.uk
www.francisfrith.co.uk

Printed and bound in Great Britain by MPG, Bodmin

Front Cover: **STAMFORD, MARKET PLACE** 1922 72298t
The colour-tinting is for illustrative purposes only, and is not intended to be historically accurate.

Frontispiece: **SKEGNESS, SOUTH PARADE** 1899 44346

AS WITH ANY HISTORICAL DATABASE THE FRITH ARCHIVE IS CONSTANTLY
BEING CORRECTED AND IMPROVED AND THE PUBLISHERS WOULD WELCOME
INFORMATION ON OMISSIONS OR INACCURACIES

LINCOLN, THE GUILDHALL 1890 / 25658

CONTENTS

FRANCIS FRITH
VICTORIAN PIONEER

Francis Frith, founder of the world-famous photographic archive, was a complex and multi-talented man. A devout Quaker and a highly successful Victorian businessman, he was philosophic by nature and pioneering in outlook. By 1855 he had already established a wholesale grocery business in Liverpool, and sold it for the astonishing sum of £200,000, which is the equivalent today of over £15,000,000. Now in his thirties, and captivated by the new science of photography, Frith set out on a series of pioneering journeys up the Nile and to the Near East.

INTRIGUE AND EXPLORATION

He was the first photographer to venture beyond the sixth cataract of the Nile. Africa was still the mysterious 'Dark Continent', and Stanley and Livingstone's historic meeting was a decade into the future. The conditions for picture taking confound belief. He laboured for hours in his wicker dark-room in the sweltering heat of the desert, while the volatile chemicals fizzed dangerously in their trays. Back in London he exhibited his photographs and was 'rapturously cheered' by members of the Royal Society. His reputation as a photographer was made overnight.

VENTURE OF A LIFE-TIME

By the 1870s the railways had threaded their way across the country, and Bank Holidays and half-day Saturdays had been made obligatory by Act of Parliament. All of a sudden the working man and his family were able to enjoy days out, take holidays, and see a little more of the world.

With typical business acumen, Francis Frith foresaw that these new tourists would enjoy having souvenirs to commemorate their days out. For the next thirty years he travelled the country by train and by pony and trap, producing fine photographs of seaside resorts and beauty spots that were keenly bought by millions of Victorians. These prints were painstakingly pasted into family albums and pored over during the dark nights of winter, rekindling precious memories of summer excursions. Frith's studio was soon supplying retail shops all over the country, and by 1890 F Frith & Co had become the greatest specialist photographic publishing company in the world, with over 2,000 sales outlets, and pioneered the picture postcard.

FRANCIS FRITH'S LEGACY

Francis Frith had died in 1898 at his villa in Cannes, his great project still growing. The archive he created continued in business for another seventy years. By 1970 it contained over a third of a million pictures showing 7,000 British towns and villages.

Frith's legacy to us today is of immense significance and value, for the magnificent archive of evocative photographs he created provides a unique record of change in the cities, towns and villages throughout Britain over a century and more. Frith and his fellow studio photographers revisited locations many times down the years to update their views, compiling for us an enthralling and colourful pageant of British life and character.

We are fortunate that Frith was dedicated to recording the minutiae of everyday life. For it is this sheer wealth of visual data, the painstaking chronicle of changes in dress, transport, street layouts, buildings, housing, engineering and landscape that captivates us so much today, offering us a powerful link with the past and with the lives of our ancestors.

Computers have now made it possible for Frith's many thousands of images to be accessed almost instantly. The archive offers every one of us an opportunity to examine the places where we and our families have lived and worked down the years. Its images, depicting our shared past, are now bringing pleasure and enlightenment to millions around the world a century and more after his death.

GRANTHAM, WESTGATE 1904 / 51631

LINCOLNSHIRE
AN INTRODUCTION

IF YOU TALK about Lincolnshire to people, as I often do (my mother was born and brought up in Gainsborough and many of my holidays were spent there in the 1950s), the flatness of the county will be the first thing mentioned. Indeed, parts of the county are flat, particularly in the south-east, in the parts of Holland bordering on the Wash. But this is not the whole picture: much of the county is rolling limestone country reaching nearly 500 feet above sea level in the south-west in the parts of Kesteven around Stamford and Grantham, with a limestone ridge running north of Lincoln to the banks of the River Humber. Further east are the Wolds, expansive chalk uplands with oceans of wheat and barley and deep-cut winding river valleys, such as those cut by the River Lymn north-west of Spilsby. These rise to over 550 feet.

Admittedly the whole of the south-east of the county is almost unrelievedly flat, with drains, dykes and canalised rivers and settlements along banks or on knolls that rise a mere few feet above the surrounding drained marshes or fens. This produces vast skies with towering clouds and long views of the higher land beyond, and the buildings thus assume greater significance. Who can forget their first long views of Lincoln Minster's three great towers atop the limestone ridge where the River Witham cuts through it, the setting sun bathing the towers and the clouds in roseate light, or the Boston Stump, that sublime church steeple, seen from the Spalding direction, or even Tattershall Castle's mighty medieval brick keep?

Amidst this great variety of landscapes are set a remarkable number of small market towns, such as Horncastle, Bourne, Spilsby and Holbeach, and small villages of every style and layout, from those such as brick-built Sutton St James that follow a dyke-top road, to warm golden oolitic limestone villages in the south-west on the edge of the Vale of Belvoir, such as Skillington. Apart from the magnificent county town of Lincoln, there are fine large towns, such as the coaching towns of Grantham and Stamford, the latter a stone-built town of the highest quality and completeness, or Boston, Louth and Spalding. There are other areas of flat country, such as the valley of the River Trent and the clay vale between the limestone ridge and the Wolds, and east of the Wolds between them and the sand-dunes of the North Sea coast. To a Lincolnshireman, the flat land only serves to make the high ground more effective. Certainly the western scarp of the Lincoln Cliff, as the limestone ridge is known north of Lincoln, or of the Lincoln Edge, as it known south of Lincoln as far south as Welbourn, is spectacularly steep; its 200 to 300 feet seem remarkably high, while from the ridge the views are vast across the Vale of Trent to the west.

As ever, the character of a county comes partly from the range of building materials from which it is forged and wrought. Lincolnshire is no exception: its character varies from the stoneless fens, where brick predominates, to the glorious stones of the south-west, the best of which is the Ancaster stone, which was widely exported for the best buildings in England. Rougher limestones are common; the stone villages extend wherever the limestone is found, such as Hemswell, east of Gainsborough. On the edge of the Wolds are greensands (often brown, rather than green), Spilsby sandstone and some chalkstone; but brick is perhaps the building material of the bulk of the county, from the great medieval buildings such as Tattershall Castle, Wainfleet School or the lodgings range of *Gainsborough's Old Hall*, down to the artisan and workers' terraces of Lincoln south of the *Witham*. Even a town like *Grantham*, on the limestone, used brick for its Georgian town houses, despite being in stone country. Timber-framing is relatively uncommon, and 'mud and stud' cottages are now distinctly rare (a light timber frame with mud walls). Unfortunately, there has been a depressing recent trend to render a lot of Lincolnshire's brick with modern 'never decorate your house again' wondercoatings, and huge numbers of older windows have been replaced by either nasty 1960s timber ones or that modern seducer of character, the plastic window.

History in Lincolnshire makes its presence felt for the first time after the Roman conquest in AD 43. What is now Lincoln was established as a legionary fortress around AD 47, for its strategic value was obvious to the Romans. The history of Lincoln itself and its transformation into 'Lindum Colonia', elided into Lincoln later on, can be found in my introduction to the companion Francis Frith Collection book 'Around Lincoln'. For the rest of what is now Lincolnshire, the Roman impact was profound: Ermine Street (not a Roman name of course) ran through the county from Stamford, where it crossed the River Well, and on to Winteringham on the River Humber, where it crossed

BELTON

BELTON HOUSE 1904 / 51644

by ferry to continue on to York. The Fosse Way, which runs from Axminster to Lincoln, enters the county north-east of Newark to merge with Ermine Street south of the city. There are other Roman roads, including King Street, which runs from Peterborough to Lincoln via Bourne, while various roads head east from Ermine Street onto and across The Wolds, one as far as Burgh le Marsh, which was then on the coast. Other important roads include the one from near Bourne into the marshes, which in Roman times were important salt-producing areas; it then headed north-west from Lincoln to cross the Trent at Littleborough, heading for Doncaster.

Besides the roads, the Romans undertook some mighty engineering works which were not equalled until Vermuyden and his Dutch compatriots in the 17th century drained the fens and the Isle of Axholme. These include Foss Dyke, a canal still in use, that linked Lincoln to the River Trent, the Sincil Dyke, and above all the Carr Dyke. This last was a banked canal dug after AD 120 to collect flood water and the rivers and streams flowing from higher ground so as to prevent flooding of the fenland. It runs from the Witham, three miles south of Lincoln, for 56 miles as far south as the River Nene, and long stretches still carry water even now. Further out the Romans embanked the coast: the road names Roman Bank in Skegness and Chapel St Leonards relate to this prodigious activity. Caistor, Ancaster and Horncastle were walled towns; stretches of Caistor's walls have been recovered by excavation, while parts of Horncastle's remain above ground. Ancaster, just north of the junction of King and Ermine Streets, has its southern earthwork defences clearly visible, while Lincoln was, of course, a walled town; part of its north gate, the Newport Arch, survives intact.

After the end of Roman occupation, the Anglo-Saxon conquerors did little reclamation in the fens and lowland marshes, but Lincolnshire became a political entity for the first time as the Anglian Kingdom of Lindsey. The genealogy of the kings survives, and the area it covered fluctuated, with the present area of the former county of Lindsey its heartland. The kingdom was absorbed by Mercia not long after AD 700, but it says much for the historical awareness of the area's traditions that when Lincolnshire emerged into the daylight of Domesday Book after the turmoil of the Danish era, the north part of the county had the name of Lindsey. It had been absorbed into the Danish colonised area, and was further sub-divided into three parts, the West, North and South Treding, the Danish word for 'third thing', thing being a council or assembly, just like Yorkshire with its Ridings or thirds. Also in Domesday Book, the south-west of the county has its own administrative area, Chetsteven, now spelt Kesteven, and Holland is also distinguishable.

This all demonstrates a remarkable historic continuity from the Anglo-Saxon to the Norman period. According to the Anglo-Saxon Chronicles, in AD 627 Lindsey was converted to Christianity by Paulinus, although it only got its first bishop in AD 678, one Eadhed. Being on the east coast, and with the Trent and Witham highly navigable, the then Mercian province of Lindsey was highly vulnerable to the longship-borne marauding armies of Danes, who are first recorded in the Chronicles as ravaging the area in AD 839. Subsequently there was considerable Danish settlement: hundreds of Danish place names can be found, particularly in the northern two-thirds of Lincolnshire. Place names ending in -by, -toft, -thorpe, and -ness, for example, abound; these include Stragglethorpe (a wonderfully ugly name), Ulceby, Wigtoft and Skegness. After Guthrum's peace with Alfred the Great in AD 886 which created the Danelaw, the whole of eastern Mercia, including its province of Lindsey, was ruled by armies based in the Five Boroughs: Stamford and Lincoln were two of them, Derby, Leicester and Nottingham the other three. Although Lincolnshire was reconquered by the English by AD 920, the Danish left an indelible imprint, together with large numbers of settlers who changed the ethnic mix for ever. Indeed, in 1013-14 Gainsborough was England's capital - Sweyn Forkbeard received the submission of the English rulers here. Sweyn died in Gainsborough on 2 February 1014 and his son, the famous King Canute, subsequently ruled England.

Lindsey's last reference in the Anglo-Saxon Chronicles ushers in a new era: in 1066, it reports that Earl Tostig, King Harold's brother, harried Lindsey and killed many good men there. Later Harold died at the Battle of Hastings, and England was conquered by William the Conqueror, Duke of Normandy. Before the Conquest there had been some major stone building, none more impressive than the minster church at Stow north-west of Lincoln, and there are many smaller churches with notable work, such as Barton-on-Humber, Hough on the Hill, Scartho and Broughton. But after the Conquest there was a great outburst of building, not only in Lincolnshire of course; but there are quite exceptionally important Norman buildings in the county. These range from the mighty westwork of Lincoln Minster or Cathedral (the seat of Remigius' bishopric transferred from far-away Dorchester on Thames), the so-called Jews' Houses in the city and St Mary's Guildhall to its south, to Boothby Pagnell manor house. Besides these crucial buildings for students of architectural history, there are numerous churches with Norman work, such as the chancel of Stow, fragments at Crowland Abbey, St Leonards Priory at Stamford and parish churches such as Whaplode or Sempringham.

The high Middle Ages were centuries of great wealth for Lincolnshire, based to a great extent on wool, and this funded some outstanding architecture. Who can forget the magnificent well-nigh architecturally perfect Boston Stump, a 15th-century tower with an early 16th-century lantern atop its 272 feet, Louth's roughly contemporary west tower and spire, totalling 295 feet in height, or Grantham's much earlier (13th-century) tower and spire 282 feet high? But these pale into insignificance beside Lincoln Minster's superlative Gothic work crowned by the sublime central and west towers; these can be seen from miles around and symbolise the importance of the city to the county. The list is long, and no-one who loves medieval churches could possibly by-pass Lincolnshire. All this reflected great wealth, and indeed the port of Boston, a new town planted around 1100, was paying more customs duties than London itself by the late 13th century. A late flowering of medieval architecture produced some superb brick buildings in areas where stone for building was rare. These include Tattershall Castle of the 1430s, Hussey's Tower in Boston, the Wainfleet School of 1484 and the 15th-century lodging ranges and tower of Gainsborough's Old Hall. For architectural heritage purposes, the decline of the county into an economic backwater with the demise of the wool trade in Tudor times preserved much more of its medieval heritage than continued economic success would have done.

By 1600 much of the county's wealth resided in agriculture, with the numerous market towns being the trade centres for their hinterlands. Great country houses replaced the abbeys, such as Thornton and Crowland, as the gentry and squirearchy built and rebuilt. Doddington Hall, Belton House, Gunby Hall, Grimsthorpe Castle, Culverthorpe Hall, Fillingham Castle and Harlaxton are a few of the survivors. Others were lost in the great country house Demolition Derby after World War II, including Bayons Manor and Tupholme Hall.

Not all Lincolnshire was agrarian, although many industries were based on agricultural products, such as the vast Maltings at Sleaford. Grimsby grew from a declined medieval port into the fifth largest in England after a new dock was built in 1800; this was followed by the arrival of the railway in 1848, and further docks came in the 1850s, including a major fish dock for the trawler fleet. Many highly advanced windmills survive, dating from the early 19th century, while brewing and malting were natural industries for such a rich agricultural county. However, only Bateman's of Wainfleet still brews. Other towns specialised in agricultural machinery, including Gainsborough, which diversified into packaging machinery. My grandfather, Wilfred Durdey, was joint managing

MABLETHORPE

THE SANDS 1890 / 26718

director of Rose Brothers in Gainsborough, whose wrapping machinery was sold world-wide. Grantham saw the first mass-produced diesel engines built in Hornsby's factory, and Lincoln had Smith's Crisps, among other industries, until the factory burned down.

On the east coast, the long sandy beaches beyond the sand dunes were seen to have potential for seaside resort development; the arrival of the railways from the Midlands in the second half of the 19th century led to their rapid, some might say under-regulated, development and their flooding with Midland day-trippers arriving by railway. Skegness started off as genteel while the Earl of Scarbrough was in control, but it soon headed for the lower end of the market. A whole string of seaside resorts grew up, from Cleethorpes in the north to Skegness via Mablethorpe, Sutton on Sea, Chapel St Leonards and Ingoldmells. Butlins built its first holiday camp at Ingoldmells in 1936, and nowadays there are vast arrays of caravan sites, amusement arcades, fun fairs and cafes to cater for trippers visiting this bracing coast.

This book is arranged in five chapters, and reflects the division of the county into three county council areas based on the historic divisions that emerged in the Middle Ages. After local government reorganisation in 1974, each of the three counties divided into two, with Lincoln as a city council. The far north was briefly merged with the East Riding of Yorkshire, but has regained its independence with the abolition of the spurious and much-hated county of Humberside. Chapter 1 tours the area of Lindsey in the north, while chapter 2 visits Lincoln and some villages round about the city. Chapter 3 tours the area of the county or 'parts' of Kesteven in the south-west, while chapter 4 follows an itinerary through the former area of the county or 'parts' of Holland. The last chapter tours the seaside resorts of the east coast in all their exuberantly cheerful splendour. The views of Skegness, however, capture a rather more sedate phase in its history. I hope you enjoy this selection of historic views and come to admire the county of Tennyson, Isaac Newton, John Wesley, William Wayneflete, Sir John Franklin, Matthew Flinders, Tony Jacklin, Ted Moult, Archbishop Whitgift and St Gilbert of Sempringham. If you are already a 'Yellow Belly', I need hardly sing the praises of Lincolnshire: you know its virtues already.

GAINSBOROUGH

MARKET PLACE c1955 / G145009

Gainsborough was briefly England's capital in 1013, when the Danish king Sweyn Forkbeard, father of King Canute, ruled. He also died and was buried here in February 1014. Here we see the 1891 Town Hall with its tottering facade shored up. A year later, in 1956, it received its present insipid Neo-Georgian frontage.

The Old Hall, very much the finest building in the town and now largely surrounded by Victorian housing, sits in its grassy square, a potent reminder of the town's great medieval past. The mansion of the mighty 15th-century De Burgh family, with a great central hall and long side wings, it is a miracle it survived, having at various times been a prison, a factory and tenements.

GAINSBOROUGH
THE OLD HALL C1955 / G145001

Behind a dry stone wall All Saints' Church sits in the centre of the winding main street of the village. Its tower dates from the 1760s; the bulk of the remainder was rebuilt in the 1860s, although there is medieval work inside, including the nave arcade.

HEMSWELL

ALL SAINTS' CHURCH C1955 / H316006

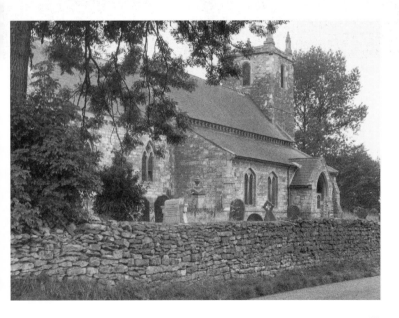

Moving east off the Limestone Cliff, our route descends towards the clay vale that runs along the western edge of The Wolds. Apart from All Saints' Church, West Rasen is noted for its 15th-century pack horse bridge which crosses the River Rase, from which the Rasens are named, and which descends from The Wolds to merge with the Ancholme to head north to the River Humber.

WEST RASEN

THE CHURCH C1955 / W379002

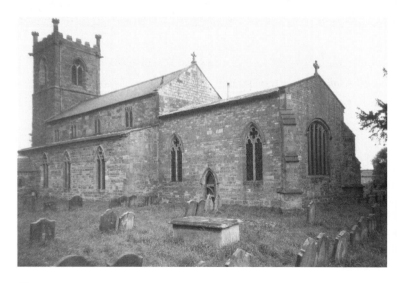

This chapter gives a snapshot of north Lincolnshire in the 1950s, as all the views were taken then: our tour takes us next to Tealby, a pretty village at the western foot of The Wolds. All Saints' Church, higher up the village, has a massive Norman tower, and the church is built in the local iron-rich brown limestone. Tealby is on the long-distance waymarked footpath which runs from the Humber to Oakham via Lincoln.

TEALBY

MARKET RASEN

QUEEN STREET c1955 / M231030

The town, separated from The Wolds to the east by thin sandy moors, now mostly afforested, became the main market for a wide area in the 16th century, and changed its name from East to Market Rasen. This view looks north towards the Market Place and captures well the character of this market town, most of whose 19th- and late 18th-century buildings still line the streets. Behind the tree on the right is the grand stone front of the old Corn Exchange built in 1854, now solicitors' offices.

Ludford is a now a single-street village on the Louth to Gainsborough road at the head of the River Bain, which flows south through the Wolds to join the River Witham. Once Ludford Parva to the west and Ludford Magna to the east, the settlements are now merged. The post office cum garage is now a house named, unsurprisingly, The Old Post Office. To the left is the churchyard wall.

LUDFORD MAGNA
THE POST OFFICE c1955 / L509010

Binbrook, on the side of a valley of the rolling western part of The Wolds north of Ludford, was once a prosperous small market town with two parish churches. This view looks north across the sloping Market Place with the parish water pump on its island protected by bollards. Now improved and the island enlarged, the lamp is now a copy of a period one.

BINBROOK

MARKET PLACE c1955 / B536006

Moving east off The Wolds, our tour reaches the flat land between them and the sea, with its high line of rolling marram-grassed sand dunes as a backdrop. Saltfleet lies just behind the dunes, but is a remnant of the medieval town and port a little further east, long washed away by the sea. North of the old windmill is the Manor House in mid 17th-century brick, which retains its original cross windows. It is said that Oliver Cromwell slept here after a Civil War skirmish at Winceby, so it would have to date from before the 1640s. The big tree has gone, and the outbuilding, whose steps can be seen at the left is now a single ruined wall.

SALTFLEET

THE MANOR HOUSE c1955 / S479011

Louth was a prosperous, compact market town serving a large area of the central Wolds. Its revival in the late 18th and early 19th centuries resulted in some fine town building and re-fronting of earlier buildings. Mercer Row is a good example, and the Georgian shop window to the right survives intact. The town is more famous, though, for its superb and grand church, crowned by its 295 feet high spire, built in the early 1500s at a cost of £305.

LOUTH

MERCER ROW c1955 / L305035

Almost swallowed up by the caravan sites to the east that merge Mablethorpe with Sutton on Sea, Trusthorpe clings to some independence. Trusthorpe Post Office is on the road to Thorpe, and is in a late Victorian projection from the left bay of a late 18th-century small farmhouse. The big tree remains, but the fence has gone and the mellow clay pantiles of the roof have been replaced.

TRUSTHORPE
THE POST OFFICE c1955 / T217010

The village lies three miles inland along what passes for a ridge in this flat country between the Wolds and the sand dunes. The church is a curious mix of greenstone and limestone giving a patchwork quilt effect, while the chancel is in brick. The 13th-century tower windows below the belfry are studded with carved dogtooth mouldings. Beyond is the school of 1874, while the foreground is now occupied by bungalows.

HUTTOFT BANK
THE CHURCH c1960 / H479301

Alford is a most attractive small market town on the eastern edge of The Wolds, noted for its thatched Manor House in West Street, a 16th-century hall house with crosswings, all encased in brick in 1661. Its market was first chartered in 1283; in this view the Market Place is beyond the medieval parish church, here partly screened by the 1906 Church Hall.

ALFORD

THE CHURCH c1955 / A209011

*At the east end of the town is Alford Mill, a six-storey, five-sail mill
built in 1813 by Sam Oxley, an Alford millwright. It is owned by
Lincolnshire County Council and has been restored to full working
order. A few windmills feature in this collection: Lincolnshire once
had over seven hundred of them.*

ALFORD

THE MILL c1955 / A209026

Dominating the Market Place is this dignified bronze statue, erected in 1861, of Sir John Franklin, the arctic explorer, born in Spilsby in 1786. His last expedition found the North–West Passage around the north of Canada, but Franklin and his crews died in 1847 when his ships, 'Erebus' and 'Terror', were trapped in the Arctic ice.

SPILSBY

THE FRANKLIN MONUMENT c1955 / S391007

Horncastle is one of the county's most ancient towns. An important medieval town, it declined until the early 19th century when the Horncastle Navigation Canal opened, giving access to Lincoln and Boston. In this view the thatched King's Head on the left and the Red Lion in the distance are 17th-century buildings amid the early 19th-century three-storey ones, which belong to that later phase of economic prosperity.

HORNCASTLE

THE BULL RING c1955 / H319020

LINCOLN

BRAYFORD POOL 1890 / 25620

Lincoln, the county town of Lincolnshire, is situated where the limestone ridge is cut through by the River Witham. Brayford Pool, a busy inland port that connected Lincoln both to the River Trent via the Roman Foss Dyke and to the sea via the Witham, is much changed now; its warehouses are mostly replaced by offices and flats, although the three on the left are the sole survivors.

The High Bridge timber-framed buildings had got into a deplorable state by the 20th century, and were extensively restored and rebuilt in 1900 by William Watkins, who also added the three dormer windows. Here we look east along the River Witham, flowing out of Brayford Pool, with the High Street reached by steps from each bank. All other buildings have been rebuilt; those on the right are the modern Marks and Spencers.

LINCOLN

THE GLORY HOLE 1906 / 55112A

LINCOLN

This view shows the ornate cast-iron balcony of the Saracen's Head Hotel, now shops, and the tower of St Peter at Arches beyond Stone Bow, built in 1720, demolished in 1933 and largely rebuilt in Lamb Gardens as St Giles's Church at the instigation of the then vicar. The statues in the niches on Stone Bow are the Archangel Gabriel and the Virgin Mary.

LINCOLN

STONE BOW 1901 / 46773

38

LINCOLN

STEEP HILL 1906 / 55115

Reaching the top of Steep Hill, the photographer looks west from Exchequer Gate, the medieval gatehouse into the cathedral close, towards the Castle gatehouse. The three-gabled and jettied timber-framed building of 1543 on the right was restored in 1929 and is now a tourist information centre. It contrasts with the fine Georgian sash-windowed building beyond.

LINCOLN

CASTLE HILL 1906 / 55115A

Inside the Castle, the photographer looks back to the gatehouse, which is basically 14th-century over a Norman archway, although the drum towers on this side are early 19th-century. The Norman castle building involved demolishing over 160 Anglo-Saxon houses; since the Middle Ages it has served as a prison and assize courts. This concludes our brief tour of Lincoln itself.

LINCOLN

THE CASTLE GATES c1955 / L49106

The stone walls of St Peter's Church, to the north of the forecourt to Doddington Hall, are a marked contrast to the mellow red brick of the Hall, which might be by Robert Smythson, the architect of Hardwick Hall. Mostly rebuilt by Thomas Lumby in the 1770s in a fairly correct Gothic, the church has a more cheery Strawberry Hill Gothick west tower and spire.

DODDINGTON

THE CHURCH 1906 / 55117

South of Lincoln a string of villages grew up along the western edge of the limestone ridge, mostly along the spring line. Navenby is a small market town with wide, airy views over the Trent valley to the west. There is a fine church, noted for its Decorated Gothic chancel, and a broad main street, once the market place. Beyond the telephone box, still here, the shop was rebuilt recently, but otherwise there has been little change.

NAVENBY

HIGH STREET C1965 / N132007

Roughly east of Navenby, where the limestone descends to the flat east of the county, Metheringham is a large village with a mix of stone and brick older houses interspersed with Victorian and later development. In this view the Beehive shop and the dormered cottage beyond survive, but the buildings beyond have been rebuilt for Townsends and the Post Office.

METHERINGHAM

HIGH STREET c1955 / M232011

Branston, around its church, has delightful winding lanes; by the church stands Hainton House of 1765, a Georgian house of some dignity. All Saints' Church is an interesting one, with Anglo-Saxon 'long and short work' quoins to the nave and an Anglo-Saxon tower with an elaborate Norman west doorway and arcading. The spire is 15th-century.

BRANSTON

THE CHURCH c1955 / B512001

WADDINGTON

To the east of Waddington is a vast Royal Air Force station, but the old village core with its mellow limestone houses and cottages remains remarkably unspoilt. The medieval church was destroyed by bombs in World War II intended for Lincoln or the RAF base, but in this view we look north past the Horse and Jockey pub in a view little changed since 1960.

East of Lincoln, Wragby is a market town on the Horncastle and
Skegness road which is very busy at weekends and in summer.
It received a market charter from Charles II, and at its centre is
a big triangular Market Place. The garage has now been replaced
by public toilets. In the distance are the Almshouses, founded by
Sir Edmund Turnor in the 17th century but rebuilt in 1840.

WRAGBY
MARKET PLACE c1965 / W382010

The parish church lies east of the Almshouses, which can be seen beyond the chancel. Built in yellow brick in 1839 in what is known as 'Commissioners Gothic', the present All Saints' was relocated by Sir Edmund Turnor to this site, a quarter of a mile away from the site of the medieval church, the chancel of which only disappeared in 1980.

WRAGBY

THE CHURCH C1965 / W382001

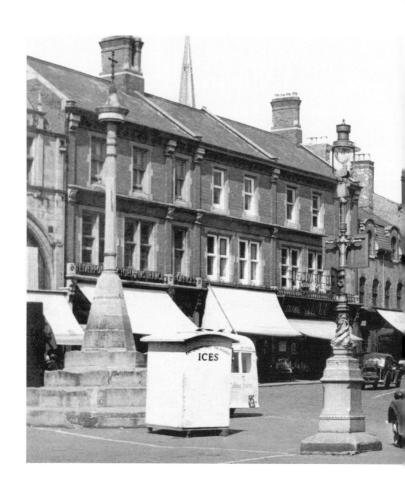

GRANTHAM

MARKET PLACE c1955 / G43034

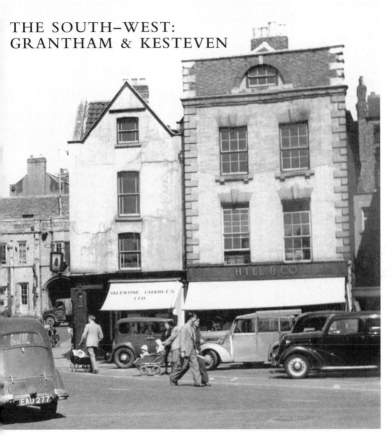

This section is a tour of the rolling oolitic limestone south-west part of Lincolnshire, until 1974 the County of Kesteven. We start in the Market Place of Grantham, a town of 30,000 whose medieval wealth was based on wool from the sheep grazing the Kesteven fields. Later an industrial town, it retains much of its Georgian and Victorian brick rebuilding of what had been a stone town.

The Angel Hotel is a remarkable late 15th-century stone-built inn, rebuilt on the site of a Knights Templar hostel where King John had held court in 1213; in this building Richard III signed the Duke of Buckingham's death warrant. The sash windows replace the original windows, although the medieval stone hood moulds survive, as do the buttresses.

GRANTHAM

THE ANGEL HOTEL 1904 / 51638

Sad to say, this is an archive view, for since 1904 all the dignified Georgian and early Victorian buildings on the right have been replaced as far as the middle distance building with a corniced parapet. More survives on the left; in the distance are the pilasters of Newton and Derry's building to give the viewer a point of reference.

GRANTHAM

HIGH STREET 1904 / 51628

At the south end of the High Street the road widens to a pleasant green, formerly a market place. At its south end is an 1891 statue of Frederick Tollemache, the town's MP for nearly 50 years from 1826. To the right is the town hall of 1867, now the Guildhall Centre, while the house to its right was replaced by a library and museum in the 1950s. To its right buildings of 1884 are now the Tollemache Inn.

GRANTHAM

ST PETER'S HILL 1904 / 51632

Back to the east of St Peter's Hill, the photographer looks north along Castlegate, with the Beehive Inn on the left; the leaves hide a beehive set in the tree, which is still there. The name sign 'East Street' has been reused on a 1960s replacement for the buildings on the right, while beyond the Gothic-style school soars the 280 feet tower and spire of St Wulfram's.

GRANTHAM

THE BEE HIVE INN 1893 / 33262

Facing the churchyard on the north side of Church Street is the oldest building in the King's School, built just before 1528 as a chantry school. This range is now the library and was, as a plaque informs us, where Isaac Newton was a pupil in the 1650s. No 1 on the right, a good 18th-century stone front, is now a Centre for Industrial Studies.

GRANTHAM

THE GRAMMAR SCHOOL 1890 / 27850

GRANTHAM

East from St Peter's Hill, Avenue Road descends towards the River Witham, lined by middle-class late Victorian semi-detached villas. There are now fewer trees, and several of the houses are offices or hotels. At the left is the rock-faced stone St Peter's Hill United Reformed Church of 1869. Many of the villas beyond are of round about that date.

Moving south from Grantham, out into the oolitic limestone country towards the Leicestershire border, we reach Skillington; it has a good range of stone houses, and a parish church with some Anglo-Saxon work in the nave and an attractive 14th-century broach spire. Far House and Tylers Farm to the left are 17th-century, while 19th-century houses are on the right.

SKILLINGTON

THE VILLAGE c1965 / S482011

This view on the Stainby Road, with the houses on the left fronting onto the High Street, which runs left from the signpost, hardly does justice to this large and attractive village in whose part-Norman parish church the great Isaac Newton was baptised. He was born in Woolsthorpe Manor, an early 17th-century house, in 1643; Woolsthorpe is a hamlet immediately north-west of the village.

COLSTERWORTH

THE VILLAGE c1960 / C428010

This is not Isaac Newton's Woolsthorpe, but the village west of Grantham in rolling countryside right on the Leicestershire border; it has fine views of Belvoir Castle a mile away on its hill on the other side of the valley of the River Devon. Further up the road is the Victorian parish church, which replaced one of 1791 which itself replaced the medieval one, apparently burned down in the Civil War.

WOOLSTHORPE

THE VILLAGE c1955 / W363020

Nearer Grantham, this gigantic Elizabethan palace is in fact 19th-century. Gregory Gregory, a bachelor, was probably responsible for as much of the design as his architects, Anthony Salvin and later William Burn, as it rose slowly throughout the 1830s and 1840s. This view is from the mile-long north-west drive: the visitor approaches a spectacularly busy mansion encrusted in turrets, bay windows, elaborate chimneys, cupolas and much more. Harlaxton Manor is now owned by the American University of Evansville.

HARLAXTON

HARLAXTON HOUSE 1890 / 22864

In the village itself, Gregory Gregory's hand is everywhere, as befits an estate village nestling at the gates of a great country house in its park. This is the school (now houses) which Gregory provided and embellished: more Tudor than the Tudors. Beneath all this timber-framing, turrets and fancy brick chimneys is an 18th-century cottage. Beyond is the crocketed spire of the church, which also received the Gregory Treatment: it is very much over-restored.

HARLAXTON

THE SCHOOLS 1890 / 22866

BELTON

*North of Grantham, set in its seven hundred acre landscaped deer park,
Belton House was begun in 1685; it is architecturally conservative for
that date with its cupola and balustraded flat roof. It was built by Sir
John Brownlow, using Lincolnshire's own superlative building stone, the
Ancaster limestone, and was acquired from the seventh Lord Brownlow by
the National Trust in 1984.*

Sleaford has fragments of a castle, built by Alexander, the princely Bishop of Lincoln, in the 1120s, but its function as a market town for north Kesteven is undimmed. This view looks north along South Gate past the extraordinarily grandiose statue in its towering medieval-style spired canopy to a 19th-century MP, Henry Handley, which dates from 1850.

SLEAFORD

THE MONUMENT c1950 / S483029

Sleaford is built on the banks of the River Slea which splits into two branches no more than streams in size. This view looks east along West Banks, with its numerous small bridges, to the mainly late Victorian artisan cottages (some are dated 1901). To the south are further artisan terraces and short side streets. The early 19th-century cottages on the left were lost in the 1960s.

SLEAFORD

WEST BANKS c1955 / S483038

*Five miles east of Sleaford, Heckington is a village widely known for its
superb 14th-century Decorated Gothic parish church with its 185 foot
high spire, rich carvings and sinuous window tracery. Here we look along
the High Street, where most of the houses and cottages survive on the left
but only No 62, then an antique shop, on the right. The village is also
known for its windmill which has no less than eight sails.*

HECKINGTON

HIGH STREET C1955 / H63003

Heading south towards Bourne, the route diverts north-east of the town to Edenham, a delightful village on the east bank of the winding East Glen River, whose church has many remarkable monuments to the Bertie family of nearby Grimsthorpe Castle. The village has mostly limestone buildings; the cedars remain in its churchyard, which is dominated by the pinnacle-topped 15th-century tower. The cottage on the right has been replaced by a stone bungalow further back from the roadside.

EDENHAM

THE VILLAGE c1955 / B511013

BOURNE

NORTH STREET 1952 / B511003

Bourne, at the junction where two Roman roads met, had a Roman station to guard the Car Dyke, the great Roman dyke 56 miles long and still surviving for long stretches. Later, Bourne became a market town with a (now largely vanished) castle and a Norman priory founded in 1138, now the parish church. Here we look from a bustling market place with the stalls spreading into North Street; the three gables of The Angel Hotel are on the left.

The Market Square is at the busy cross-roads in the centre of this delightful small town. The Gothic-style drinking fountain of 1860 has been relocated to the cemetery in South Road, presumably to save it from the traffic, while the good stone-tile-roofed building beyond on the corner of South Street is still Harrison and Dunn's shop today.

BOURNE
MARKET SQUARE c1955 / B511002

Stamford, one of England's most attractive and historic towns, is only just in Lincolnshire. The River Welland is the boundary between it and Northamptonshire. This view from the water meadows is a very well known one and relatively little changed, although it would look very different to a late medieval traveller when there were fourteen parish church towers in this view.

STAMFORD
FROM THE WATER MEADOWS 1922 / 72296

Much of 18th-century Stamford's trade came from its location on the Great North Road, and it had numerous coaching inns. The George is probably the best known, an inn since 1568 and noted for its sign spanning the road. Beyond is part of Lord Burghley's Hospital, then the river, and up the hill in Stamford proper the elegant 160 foot tower and spire of St Mary's Church, a superb 13th-century Early English Gothic structure.

STAMFORD

THE GEORGE HOTEL 1922 / 72305

STAMFORD

ST MARY'S STREET 1922 / 72309

STAMFORD

MARKET PLACE 1922 / 72298

This view looks north towards All Saints' Church, whose massive tower and elegant crocketted spire dominate its battlemented nave, chancel and aisles. To its right Barn Hill climbs gently north-west, a street of almost unspoilt Georgian houses.

STAMFORD

RED LION SQUARE 1922 / 72299

Our photographer now proceeds east along the High Street, a relatively narrow street with a mix of 17th-century and later fronts, now pedestrianised. The gabled Grant's butcher's shop has been removed to the Kirkgate Museum in York, Singer's has lost its elegant shopfronts and has been texture-coated, and Star Stores opposite was rebuilt in rough replica in 1982 for The Halifax.

STAMFORD

HIGH STREET 1922 / 72302

THE SOUTH-EAST:
BOSTON & THE FLAT
COUNTRY OF HOLLAND

MARKET DEEPING

THE MARKET PLACE 1900 / M116301

This section takes a tour from east of Stamford into the fenland of Lincolnshire, mostly in the former administrative county of Holland, very much the flat country. As its name implies, Market Deeping is a market town with a large, triangular market place, lined with pubs such as the Bull for the farmers and coaching inns for travellers, including the Deeping Stage on the left and the King's Head Inn on the right.

Church Street is much quieter, away from the A16 Stamford to Spalding road. Another wide street, and also laid out as a market, it has many good stone houses, including almshouses of 1877 on the left and several pubs. The view along the grass-verged straight street is closed by the dignified 15th-century tower of St Guthlac's Church.

MARKET DEEPING

CHURCH STREET c1955 / M116007

East of Market Deeping and joined to it is Deeping St James village. At its heart is this curious structure in medieval stone. The former village cross, it was built in the 15th century, but in 1819 the cross shaft was removed and the base, quite extraordinarily, was converted into the village lock-up. Looking north-west past the village cross, we see the church with its curiously plain tower and mean spire. Closer examination reveals that the tower was in fact built in 1717 in a version of Gothic that fails to convince. Inside, by contrast, the late 12th-century nave arcades are serene and perfectly proportioned, as befits a church owned by the mighty Thorney Abbey.

DEEPING ST JAMES
THE CHURCH AND THE CROSS c1965 / D150001

The town grew up at the gates of the abbey on a low island amid the surrounding marshes, receiving its charter in 1142. Apart from the Abbey, the town is famous for the 14th-century triangular bridge, seen here from West Street. The streets now no longer have streams flowing down them, so the bridge is a redundant curiosity in a town with many good things architecturally.

CROWLAND

THE BRIDGE 1894 / 34833

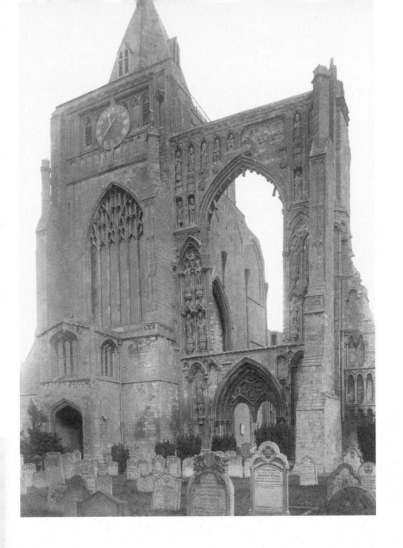

CROWLAND

THE ABBEY 1894 / 34831

Reaching Spalding we are in the heart of the bulb-growing country; the surrounding countryside is a glorious carpet of daffodils, tulips and other flowers at different times of the year. This view looks west on market day. The White Hart Hotel's stuccoed front dates from about 1714. It is currently closed. The Natwest bank to its right is over-scaled 1930s Neo-Georgian, while to the left of the White Hart two buildings have recently also been replaced in pallid Neo-Georgian.

SPALDING

MARKET PLACE c1955 / S388171

Spalding's townscape is 'made' by the River Welland, which bisects the town. There are roads along each bank and houses face the river, giving it a slightly Dutch feel. Indeed, there are some fine Georgian houses, particularly on the east side near the good parish church. Here we look towards High Bridge of 1838. Berrills and the buildings beyond have been demolished to make way for road improvements and a riverside walk.

SPALDING

HIGH BRIDGE c1960 / S388227

Moving east along B-roads zig-zagging through the Fens, we reach Long Sutton. This market town is noted for its rare 13th-century lead spire and late Norman nave. In the Market Place at first sight all looks broadly unchanged, but since 1950 the Bull has been entirely rebuilt in rough replica, and the Crown and Woolpack has had its stucco removed, but the chemist's shop is still a chemist, albeit no longer run by Norman Hounslow.

LONG SUTTON
MARKET PLACE c1950 / L484011

West of Long Sutton and east of Spalding, Holbeach is another of Lincolnshire's numerous small market towns. It received its first market charter in 1252. The north side of High Street, on the right, has some dignified late 18th- and early 19th-century three-storey houses, including the Bell and the Chequers Hotels. On the left is the churchyard, and beyond is an Italianate building of the 1890s that plays a major townscape role.

HOLBEACH

HIGH STREET c1955 / H318016

Further east, Franklins Outfitters, a mid 19th-century Italianate building on the right has gone, as have those in the distance on the left, to be replaced by the tepid Neo-Georgian Talbot Court. The 180-foot spire of All Saints' can be seen beyond, but the most remarkable feature of the church is the north porch: this seems to be a re-used castle gatehouse, perhaps from Moulton Castle, five miles to the west.

HOLBEACH
HIGH STREET C1955 / H318015

Heading towards Boston, we reach Donington on the Grantham to Boston road, an attractive market town, once the centre of a flax and hemp trade with three hemp fairs a year. This view looks east from the Market Place along the High Street, not the most distinguished in Lincolnshire; however, the Red Cow is a coaching inn with an 18th-century refront to a 17th-century inn and has a former assembly room to its right.

DONINGTON

HIGH STREET c1965 / D220020

Boston, Botolph's Town, was laid out along the banks of the River Witham some time around 1100, within the parish of nearby Skirbeck, and rapidly became a great port, although it only received its first charter in 1205 from King John. It acquired town walls in 1285, and in 1353 it wrested away Lincoln's wool staple. It was the wool trade that built the town, with its seething market and vast numbers of ships.

BOSTON

MARKET PLACE 1899 / 43295

The town centre is dominated by its very large triangular market place, which in its turn is visually overwhelmed by the mighty church steeple, completed in 1460 and universally known as the Boston Stump. Crowned by an octagonal lantern, it soars 272 feet above the town and can be seen from miles around, even from Lincoln. It served as a landmark for shipping, for the lantern used to have a beacon lit at night.

In South Street, Shodfriars Hall is an echo of the four friaries established in the medieval town. In fact it was probably the hall of a trade guild, but in its present form it owes more to John Oldrid Scott's 'restoration' in 1874 than the Middle Ages. It probably had an open ground storey for trade, rather like Thaxted's Guildhall in Essex, but it is a splendid reminder of the town's medieval past.

BOSTON

SHODFRIARS HALL 1889 / 22274

Further south, High Street opens up to the river, the buildings terminating in an elegant early 19th-century five-storey warehouse with a hipped roof: more like a very tall villa than a warehouse. The warehouses of Boston have suffered in recent years; the ones on the right on the opposite bank have been converted into flats, but the distant one has been, like so many of its companions, demolished.

BOSTON
DOUGHTY QUAY 1890 / 26066

BOSTON

TOWER STREET 1893 / 32065

Battle your way across or round the inner relief road that did so much damage to the town's historic fabric and cross the Maud Foster Drain into Willoughby Road, where Boston's celebrated Maud Foster Mill dominated the town's eastern growth beyond the town walls. Built in 1819, this five sailer, in working order, now has tea rooms in the mill warehouse whose weatherboarded bag hoist turret is visible between now-demolished houses.

BOSTON

THE WINDMILL C1965 / B155096

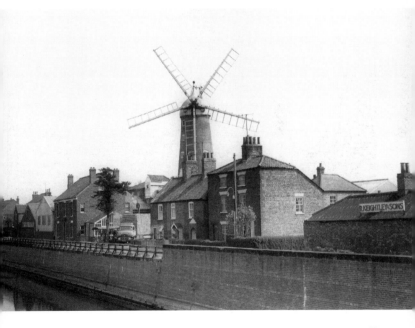

Built south of the town, the new docks were 825 feet long by 450 feet wide and are still busy. However, none of the buildings survive, although the dock walls and the entrance abutments in the distance remain. Boston's Tudor decline was steep: the wool trade upon which the town had waxed fat faded away, and the river silted up. It was not until the 18th century that the town recovered, and the railway arrived in 1848. A new dock was authorised by Act of Parliament in 1881 and was opened in 1882, partly paid for by the Great Northern Railway, who extended a branch line to it.

BOSTON

THE DOCKS 1890 / 32078

CONINGSBY

THE MILL c1955 / C429003

Heading north-west roughly parallel to the River Witham, we reach two small towns on either side of the River Bain, which meets the Witham a mile away at Dogdyke. Coningsby, on the south bank, has lost much of its historic character: in this view of Silver Street the house in front of the mill survives, but not the mill; all to the left has gone, and the road at the right has become a footpath.

Across the Bain, Tattershall is altogether less ravaged by 1960s and later rebuilding. Due to the lack of building stone in this part of the county, brick made an early appearance; several major medieval brick buildings survive. We have already seen the Hussey Tower in Boston, while Lord Cromwell's mighty brick tower keep of the 1430s can be seen for miles across the flat Fens of Holland.

TATTERSHALL

THE CASTLE c1955 / T15025

The town was probably established as a port on the Wainfleet Haven by Bardney Abbey, but by the 15th century the haven silted up and the port declined. The Haven became a continuation of the Steeping River, and the sea is now three miles away. At its centre is the square Market Place with a medieval market cross whose shaft can be seen to the left.

WAINFLEET ALL SAINTS

MARKET PLACE C1955 / W550002

*Back in the Market Place, the photographer looks south down the High
Street. Cook's on the corner is still a newsagent and stationer, Goodnews.
On the right are the two best pubs architecturally in the town, the Red
Lion and the Angel Inn.*

WAINFLEET ALL SAINTS

HIGH STREET c1955 / W550007

North of Wainfleet, on the Skegness to Lincoln road, Burgh le Marsh is a market town whose charter was granted in 1401. At its east end is another of Lincolnshire's preserved windmills. Built in 1813 by Oxley of Alford, it is a five-sailer owned by the County Council and often open to the public. The main road lies beyond the mill and the meadow remains unbuilt on, while the mill buildings also survive.

BURGH LE MARSH
THE WINDMILL c1955 / B513020

SKEGNESS

THE PIER 1899 / 44350

SEASIDE
LINCOLNSHIRE

Skegness owed its popular success to the railway, which reached here in 1873 as an extension from the then terminus at Wainfleet. There had been a middle-class watering place attached to what was little more than a fishing village. A new town was laid out from 1876 by the Earl of Scarbrough; in 1881 it acquired a splendid pier, seen here and unrecognisable to the modern visitor.

Skegness was very much developed with day trips and excursions in mind, utilising the railway, with influxes from the Midlands, particularly Nottingham. Here we see the funfair actually on the sands above the high water mark, including a helter-skelter tower. It was not until 1921, when the council bought the sea -front and foreshore from the Earl, that the town assumed its brasher kiss-me-quick character.

SKEGNESS

FROM THE PIER 1910 / 62843

In 1978 the section of the pier between the concert hall at the
end, from which this view was taken, was destroyed in storms.
The landward end of the 1840 foot long pier had already been
submerged in 1970 by the enclosed Skegness Pier Amusements,
although some of the original structure can be seen at the sea end.
This view shows the resort still in its genteel phase under the Earl
of Scarbrough's strict control.

SKEGNESS

THE PIER 1899 / 44194

A vital landmark building in trying to relate these early views to present-day Skegness is the Jubilee Clock Tower, erected at the junction of Lumley Road with the then seafront's Grand Parade and South Parade. The Tower was built to commemorate Queen Victoria's Diamond Jubilee: this view was taken on 11 August 1899, and shows its formal opening by the Countess of Scarbrough.

SKEGNESS

GRAND PARADE AND THE CLOCK TOWER 1899 / 44195

The garlands from the formal opening are still evident in this view, in which visitors admire the pristine stone and brick of the Clock Tower. In the distance is the pier, a view now wholly obscured by the enormous funfair, while the front gardens to the sea front villas have long gone.

SKEGNESS
THE SEAFRONT 1899 / 44197

This view looks towards the Jubilee Clock Tower, with Lumley Road to its left. The buildings on the left survive, now with large shops built out at ground floor level, but the corner building on the north side of Lumley Road, to the left of the Clock Tower, has been (badly) replaced in the 1960s.

SKEGNESS

THE PARADE 1899 / 44346

SKEGNESS

THE BEACH 1910 / 62865

The acres and acres of superb sand are what make these Lincolnshire coastal resorts such a pleasure; I remember donkey rides here, and indeed my daughters have also ridden the Skegness donkeys in the past. Here we look beyond the licensed donkey ride man, the helter-skelter and beach fun fair, the bathing machines and the booths towards the then splendid pier.

Skegness's most famous fairground ride was the Figure Eight, which was regarded as a worthy rival to Coney Island! No doubt it looks tame to the present generation reared on the terrors of Alton Towers, but to a boy in the 1950s it was quite scary enough. It is now replaced by an altogether more testing version as part of the Pleasure Beach complex.

SKEGNESS

THE FIGURE EIGHT 1910 / 62862

At the west end of Lumley Road there were a few shops in 1899, but the view is utterly transformed now from Roman Bank, a reference to the old Roman sea wall. The charmingly rustic stone lion at the left has been replaced by a corner turret and all the buildings are now shops, many of which have been rebuilt, but the view is still terminated by the Jubilee Clock Tower.

SKEGNESS

LUMLEY ROAD 1899 / 44354

Before you reach Ingoldmells, north of Skegness, you pass one of Butlins' large holiday camps. Indeed, it was Billy Butlin's very first one, opened in 1936 and the first in the country. In this view we see the rather good Art Deco 'Butlins Ingoldmells Hotel', now brutally changed. The central stone-faced pavilion has now been lowered and clad in profiled metal sheeting, while the ground floor openings have been infilled. To complete the aesthetic devastation, the whole thing has been painted pale grey except for a band of brickwork.

INGOLDMELLS
BUTLINS HOLIDAY CAMP c1955 / I47026

Here, looking towards Ingoldmells Point, are the sandy beach and the sand dunes, a view now radically changed by the more recent sea defences with a massive concave-fronted sea wall forming a promenade. Inland, Ingoldmells is very much kiss-me-quick hat country, with vast caravan parks, amusement arcades and a fun fair whose piece de resistance is the Volcano.

INGOLDMELLS

VICKERS POINT AND THE BEACH c1955 / I47005

To the north beyond Ingoldmells, and rather more genteel, is Chapel St Leonards, where my mother used to holiday in the 1930s. This view is taken from the sandy Roman Bank path looking to Chapel Point. The breakwaters have gone and the sea wall has been rebuilt, but most of the beach huts remain, with quaint names like Dolly's Den, Molly's and Sand Lea.

CHAPEL ST LEONARDS

CHAPEL POINT c1955 / c427301

Eight miles further north along the coast is Sutton on Sea, another seaside resort somewhat overshadowed by Mablethorpe, the two linked by caravan sites. The promenade seen here was built in the 1880s at a cost of £350, but it was destroyed in the catastrophic 1953 floods. The pier beside the two ladies, one with an umbrella, is all that survives; it is known as the Lion Pillar.

SUTTON ON SEA
THE BEACH 1890 / 26695

Sutton on Sea's parish church, St Clement's, is Lincolnshire's very own Leaning Tower of Pisa, doubtless owing to its sandy foundations having settled since it was built in 1819. There is medieval stonework in the nave, but the church is mainly 1819 brick with an 1860 chancel. The 1819 churchwardens took no chances: it was built inland, the original medieval one having been washed away by the sea.

SANDILANDS

THE CROOKED CHURCH c1955 / S480042

Here we see the post-1953 sea wall, stepped here to allow access to the beach. The cafe and snack bar have now been rebuilt, but the beach is as busy as ever with day trippers from Lincolnshire and further afield on any sunny weekend day.

INDEX

PLEASE HELP US BRING FRITH'S
PHOTOGRAPHS TO LIFE

Our authors do their best to recount the history of the places they write about. They give insights into how particular towns and villages developed, they describe the architecture of streets and buildings, and they discuss the lives of famous people who lived there. But however knowledgeable our authors are, the story they tell is necessarily incomplete.

Frith's photographs are so much more than plain historical documents. They are living proofs of the flow of human life down the generations. They show real people at real moments in history; and each of those people is the son or daughter of someone, the brother or sister, aunt or uncle, grandfather or grandmother of someone else. All of them lived, worked and played in the streets depicted in Frith's photographs.

We would be grateful if you would tell us about the many places shown in our photographs—the streets with their buildings, shops, businesses and industries. Describe your own memories of life in those streets: what it was like growing up there, who ran the local shop and what shopping was like years ago; if your workplace is shown tell us about your working day and what the building is used for now. With your help more and more Frith photographs can be brought to life, and vital memories preserved for posterity.

We will gradually add your comments and stories to the archive for the benefit of historians of the future. Wherever possible, we will try to include some of your comments in future editions of our books. Moreover, if you spot errors in dates, titles or other facts, please let us know, because our archive records are not always completely accurate—they rely on 150 years of human endeavour and hand-compiled records.

So please write, fax or email us with your stories and memories. Thank you!

FREE PRINT OF YOUR CHOICE

Choose any Frith photograph in this book.
Simply complete the Voucher opposite and
return it with your remittance for £2.25 (to
cover postage and handling) and we will print
the photograph of your choice in SEPIA (size
11 x 8 inches) and supply it in a cream mount
with a burgundy rule line
(overall size 14 x 11 inches).

**Please note: photographs with a reference number
starting with a "Z" are not Frith photographs and
cannot be supplied under this offer.**

Offer valid for delivery to UK one address only.

Mounted Print
Overall size 14 x 11 inches (355 x 280mm)

PLUS: **Order additional Mounted Prints at
HALF PRICE - £7.49 each** (normally £14.99)
If you would like to order more Frith prints
from this book, possibly as gifts for friends and
family, you can buy them at half price (with no
additional postage and handling costs).

PLUS: **Have your Mounted Prints framed**
For an extra £14.95 per print you can have your
mounted print(s) framed in an elegant polished
wood and gilt moulding, overall size
16 x 13 inches (no additional postage and
handling required).

IMPORTANT!

These special prices are only
available if you use this form to
order. You must use the ORIGINAL
VOUCHER (no copies permitted).

We can only despatch to one
UK address. This offer cannot be
combined with any other offer.

FRITH PRODUCTS AND SERVICES

All Frith photographs are available for you to buy as framed or mounted prints.
From time to time, other illustrated items such as Address Books and Maps are also
available. Already, almost 80,000 Frith archive photographs can be viewed and
purchased on the internet through the Frith website.

For more detailed information on Frith companies and products, visit:

www.francisfrith.co.uk

For further information, or trade enquiries, contact:

The Francis Frith Collection, Frith's Barn, Teffont, Salisbury SP3 5QP

Tel: +44 (0) 1722 716 376 Fax: +44 (0) 1722 716 881 Email: sales@francisfrith.co.uk